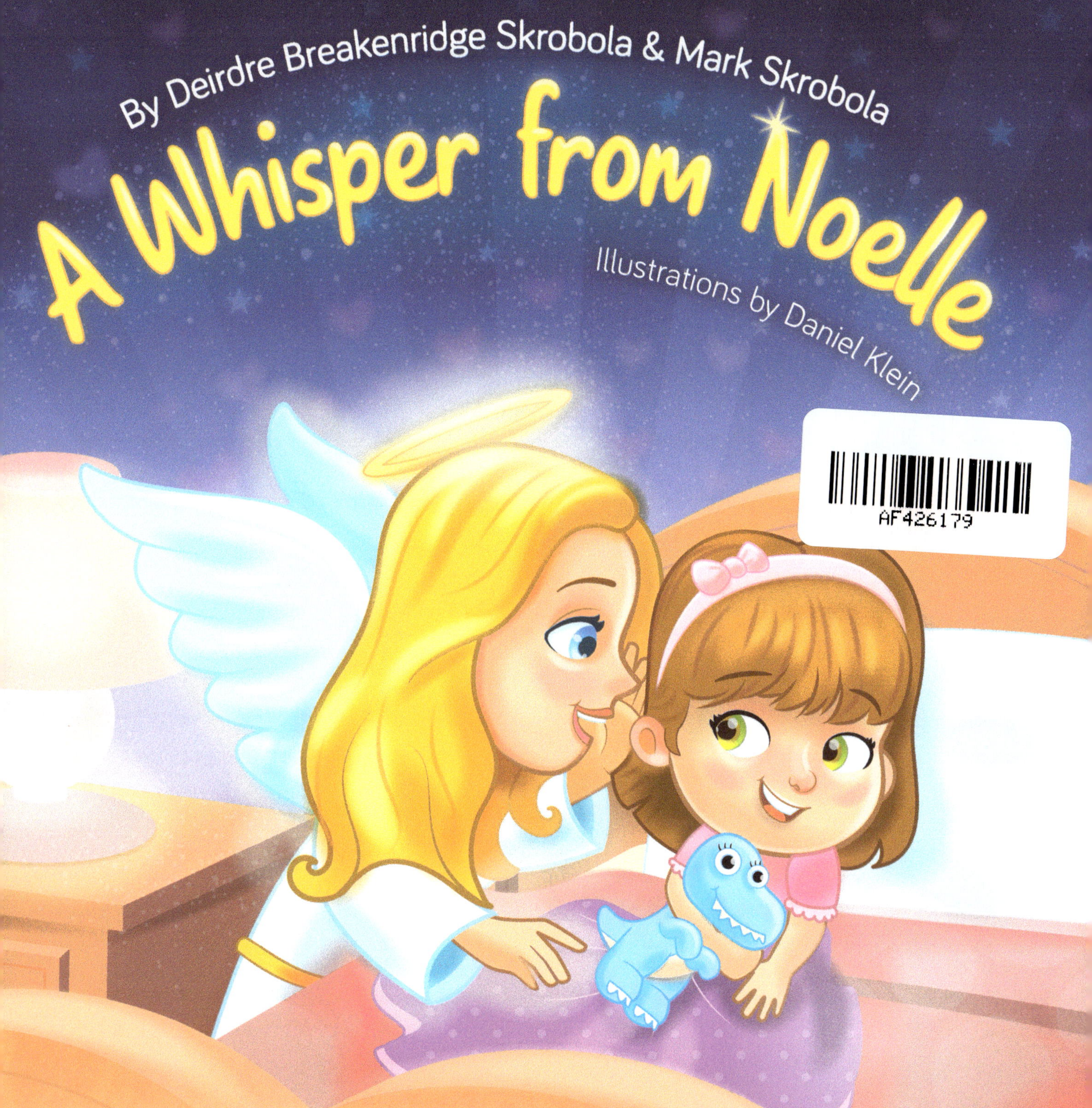

By Deirdre Breakenridge Skrobola & Mark Skrobola
A Whisper from Noelle
Illustrations by Daniel Klein
AF426179

This Whisper belongs to

____

To our angel Noelle...
Forever in our hearts.

"Last night an angel came to me when I was lying in my bed," said Ashley-Ann as she snuggled closer to her mommy.

"What did the angel look like, honey?"

"She was the most beautiful girl I've ever seen, with blonde hair and big blue eyes."

Her mom smiled warmly. "What did she want?"
"I think she wanted me to know that it's okay to be me."
Ashley-Ann gave her mommy a big hug.

"What was the angel's name?"
Beaming with delight, Ashley-Ann said,
"Her name was Noelle."

Ashley-Ann remembered the message from Noelle. It was a gentle and kind message. Just a whisper. Yet it came through to her loud and clear.

That night, Noelle spoke softly into Ashley-Ann's ear: "You're everything and more, and you're very special."

Her voice sounded like a song whistling in the wind. "If you can walk through this world feeling kindness and warmth, and with love in your heart, then you will always smile and be happy."

In Ashley-Ann's mind, Noelle's message formed a word she had heard before. It was "feel."

Noelle came to Ashley-Ann with this important message. She wanted Ashley-Ann to know that she should always share her true feelings. Because when you are able to feel, you share a big part of yourself with the people you love. When you can feel, then others will do the same.

Ashley-Ann wasn't exactly sure she understood what Noelle was saying. She asked, "What does it mean to feel?"

Once again, Noelle whispered to Ashley-Ann, "When you feel, that means you can be happy and free from anything that frightens you. You face your fears. When you share what scares you, then you can get the help and the care you need from your mommy and daddy and others who love you."

Noelle also wanted Ashley-Ann to know that she should always be kind and have compassion for others. She said, "If you feel deeply for others, then you can help them to feel warmth and kindness. Together, you'll experience something very special with the people who mean the most in your life."

Noelle went on to tell Ashley-Ann that it was also important for her always to tell the truth—to be true to others and also be true to herself. Ashley-Ann looked at Noelle and remembered, "Mommy always says I should tell the truth. But what does it mean to be true to yourself?"

Noelle smiled and said, "Yes, your mommy is right…you should always tell the truth. Being true to yourself means trusting what you feel can be good and right for you. There's a little voice inside of you that will tell you what feels good and right, and what feels wrong. You may not know this voice now. However, someday, you will know exactly what I mean."

No no no...
don't do that.

There was one last thing Noelle whispered before she left Ashley-Ann that night. "When you feel, you can love with all your heart, and you let others love you back."

Ashley-Ann said, "How will I know that I'm able to love and that others love me?"

Noelle asked her quietly, "When you think of the word 'love,' who pops into your mind, and how do you feel?"

Ashley-Anne said, "I think of my mommy and daddy, and I feel really happy."

"Well, then, that's how you'll know." Noelle kissed Ashley-Ann on the forehead and then left as quickly as she came.

As Ashley-Ann was remembering her conversation with Noelle, she smiled at her mommy and said, "I feel happy, and I love you."

Her mom held her close and said, "I love you more.
Tell me something, where is Noelle now?"

Ashley-Ann paused for a moment and looked up toward the sky and said, "Noelle is really far away. Yet I feel like she's still so close to me. I'll never forget what Noelle whispered, and I'll always feel her in my heart."

The end

FEEL
F = Face your Fears
E = Have Empathy for Others
E = Live with Ethics and Good Judgment
L = Unleash your Love

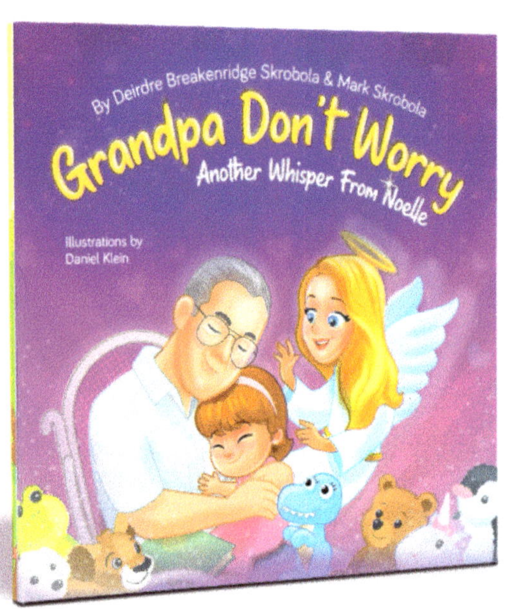

Grandpa Don't Worry

One night, Ashley-Ann receives a very special visit from her friend, an angel named Noelle. In a series of whispers, Ashley-Ann listens closely to hear important messages that she needs to share with her grandpa. Through Noelle, Ashley-Ann discovers that Grandpa has feelings too. He sometimes worries. He wants Ashley-Anne to understand the importance of family values, which include love, strength, caring, and kindness.

Knowing that Ashley-Ann learns about these "Loving Lessons" from Noelle, makes her Grandpa very happy. With these caring messages, children and families can explore feelings and values together and what it means to be kind and to understand each other. This insightful story is sure to be a favorite among readers of all ages.

Daddy Are You Listening

While walking in the park one day, Ashley-Ann is not sure her daddy listens to her. She shares the week's exciting events, and his mind is elsewhere. Ashley-Ann remembers that her friend, Noelle, an angel, recently visited and whispered an important message in her ear. Noelle told Ashley-Ann that her daddy was trying to listen, and she needed to help him. That day in the park, Ashley-Ann learned how to help her daddy be a better listener and what it means to listen to each other. Children and families can explore feelings and values with this caring message. Listening is the first step to caring, kindness, and showing you understand the ones you love. This insightful story will be a favorite among readers of all ages.

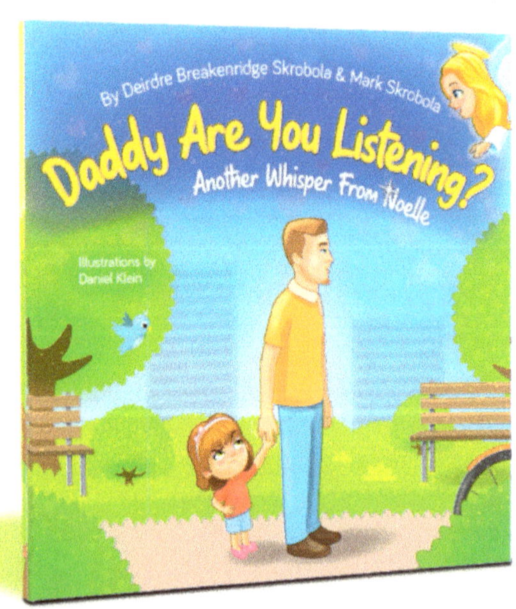

www.ingramcontent.com/pod-product-compliance
Lightning Source LLC
Chambersburg PA
CBHW040221110726

48005CB00019B/3111